CLOISTER

BOOKS

Cloister Books are inspired by the monastic custom of walking slowly and reading or meditating in the monastery cloister, a place of silence, centering, and calm. Within these pages you will find a similar space in which to pray and reflect on the presence of God.

Crossing the Jordan

Crossing the Jordan

ಅ ಅ ಅ

Meditations on Vocation

Sam Portaro

COWLEY PUBLICATIONS
Cambridge · Boston
Massachusetts

Published in the United States of America by Cowley
Publications, a division of the Society of St. John the
Evangelist. No portion of this book may be reproduced,
stored in or introduced into a retrieval system, or transmit-
ted, in any form or by any means—including photocopy-
ing—without the prior written permission of Cowley
Publications, except in the case of brief quotations embodied in critical articles and reviews.

Library of Congress Cataloging-in-Publication Data:
Portaro, Sam Anthony.
    Crossing the Jordan: meditations on vocation
    by Sam Portaro.
        p.   cm.
    ISBN 1-56101-170-3 (alk. paper)
    1. Vocation—Christianity. I. Title.
BV4740.P67   1999
248.4—dc21   99-40384
                                              CIP
    Scripture quotations are taken from *The New Revised
    Standard Version* of the Bible, © 1989, by the Division
    of Christian Education of the National Council of the
    Churches of Christ in the United States of America.
    Used by permission.

Cynthia Shattuck, editor; Annie G. Kammerer, copyeditor;
Vicki Black, cover and interior design
Cover art: *Kasaner* (1968) by Kenzo Okada
This book was printed in Canada on recycled, acid-free
paper.

Cowley Publications
28 Temple Place   •   Boston, Massachusetts 02111
800-225-1534   •   http://www.cowley.org

For Christopher,
who was waiting on the other side of my Jordan

☙

Table of Contents

ॐ

Acknowledgments

This project owes its life to an earlier one. Craig
Dykstra and James Wind, through their offices
with the Lilly Endowment, encouraged me to explore
young adult vocation and enabled me to do so with a
generous grant that culminated in another, earlier
book. Gary Peluso, my able co-author on that project,
was a constant conversation partner whose questions
often led me to deeper insights. I had a "silent
partner," too, an author whose scholarly writings
provoked me to see the gospels anew. I am much
indebted to John Dominic Crossan, whose influence
pervades these meditations.

While my thoughts were focused on themes of
vocation, I led a retreat for students from the
University of Chicago in February 1992, the first

group to encounter many of the thoughts woven in this text. We met at the DeKoven Center in Racine, Wisconsin, the site of the first student conferences hosted in 1926 by Edna Biller that became, through her founding in 1929, our present ministry at Brent House.

In March of the same year I shared the same material as a Quiet Day for the Daughters of the King and the Brotherhood of St. Andrew of the Diocese of Chicago at the church of St. Raphael the Archangel in Oak Lawn, Illinois. And in November 1992 I offered the original meditations as The Lichtenberger Lectures at Thompson Center in St. Louis, Missouri. Presenting these ideas to and discussing them with these communities of varied ages and perspectives suggested that these themes were of broader interest and applicable beyond the experience of young adulthood. I am grateful to them all for their encouragements.

I am deeply indebted to Cynthia Shattuck at Cowley Publications. Her continuing nurture of my ideas, and her guidance in their organization and timely presentation to others, are invaluable to one whose writing must be balanced with the many tasks of modern ministry on a major campus.

Acknowledgments

Vicki Black and Annie Kammerer, my editors, make me look far better than I am and know my errors all too well; and Jennifer Hopcroft understands that marketing is a ministry. To them all I am grateful, for without them, I'd have never met you, the reader.

Lastly, I thank God for my families—the immediate circle who gave me life, nurtured me, and never fails to love me; that extended community of the church within whose company I've spent the better part of life's journey; and Chris Dionesotes, my partner in every sense of the word.

‰

Introduction

This extended meditation began as a set of shorter ruminations for a student retreat. I was encouraged by those who attended that event to repeat the same meditations with different retreatants, of diverse age and experience, on two more occasions. Requests for copies of the original texts suggested that my thoughts were helpful to others who were exploring their vocational journeys.

It has been nearly a decade since I first set down these themes. In the intervening years I have written several books, including, with Gary Peluso, *Inquiring and Discerning Hearts: Vocation and Ministry with Young Adults on Campus*. This book is a sequel to that one, an attempt to wrestle with the angel of vocation. In more than twenty years of ministry on campus, among young adults and older ones, too, I find that vocation is the central and enduring theme—the tie that binds, and sometimes chafes.

I have returned to these ruminations many times: in conversations, in sermons, in counsel. In this version, I have chosen to share more autobiographical detail. In part, I have done this out of consideration for the reader who, having no prior relationship with me, would be denied much of the personal context that those first students from my community knew and understood. But I have also included some of my own story because I have come to believe that this is one of our primary obligations as witnesses to a faith heritage that is itself the collected stories of the vocational journeys of our spiritual forebears.

I have dared to eisegete their scriptures; I have read between the lines. For I now realize that this intuitive interpretive reading is part of our knowing one another, and knowing ourselves. Hence, the popularity of biography: in the stories and experiences of others we find insights into ourselves, and companionship on life's journey. These meditations are a companion to the gospels. References are included as encouragement to draw closer to Jesus as the gospellers, and countless others, encountered him. The gospels, while not exclusively biographies of Jesus or of their authors, do contain biographical elements. Like biography, what the gospels tell us about Jesus invites reflection: what we hear, read, see, and even experience of another must always be subjected to thoughtful scrutiny, a discipline one psychologist calls "listening with the third ear." Thus I have "listened" to the stories of Jesus' life with a "third ear," attuned to find resonances with my own life experience, and the experiences I have been privileged to share through the vocational journeys of so many others.

As I write these words, I am in the mountains of North Carolina in the midst of more than a thousand students and campus ministry colleagues at a conference—a retreat of sorts. Ironically, coincidentally, and providentially, I am literally in the place where much of my own story was shaped, among many of my companions in that way, engaged in the very activity of discernment which I have written about in these pages. It seems a holy, harmonic convergence. Therefore, I give thanks for this place, for these people, for this ministry, and offer these chapters out of gratitude to the God who made them all and has so generously shared them with me.

You are the salt of the earth....You are the light of the world. A city built on a hill cannot be hid. No one after lighting a lamp puts it under the bushel basket, but on the lampstand, and it gives light to all in the house. In the same way, let your light shine before others, so that they may see your good works and give glory to your Father in heaven.

(Matthew 5:13, 14-16)

∂
1

Getting a Life

U ncle Buddy died yesterday. His death was swift
and unexpected—an aneurysm on the aorta.
Two more years and he would have retired. Buddy was
Aunt Peggy's husband, or more correctly, her widow-
er. Aunt Peggy, Mama's younger sister, died about
eight years ago after a long and painful battle with
cancer.

I remember when they married. I was just beginning school. But since Mama, Daddy, my two brothers
and I were all living with my Mama's parents, we were
all caught up in the wedding stuff. Aunt Peggy was
sweet. She was a hairdresser and all her customers
loved her. She loved Persian cats, sweet desserts, and

had a laugh that was hearty, lilting, and infectious all at the same time. Through a torturously painful and protracted illness that consumed the last years of her life, she never complained, but even apologized that her condition inconvenienced others. When she died, the sun of our lives dimmed.

Uncle Buddy was a mystery. He never said much. But he and Aunt Peggy seemed to get along. Oh, there was occasional talk of some tensions—half-whispered adult family conversations that died suddenly when any of us children drew within earshot—but they never amounted to anything. My cousin Sharon was their only child, same age as my sister Karen. Sharon and Karen both delivered healthy babies last spring. Uncle Buddy was hesitant to hold his new granddaughter—perhaps afraid he'd be too clumsy. His hands were used to heavier work. He was employed by one of the many furniture manufacturers in High Point, North Carolina. That's all I ever knew of his work; just that it was in furniture, and in the hands-on making of it.

Whenever the family gathered, Buddy was the quietest one. But he was not without the capacity to surprise. I don't think I was the only one who noticed that after Aunt Peggy's death Buddy carefully tended her roses. And every year at Christmas I got a card, addressed and signed "Love, Uncle Buddy" in a beautiful flowing script as perfect as Aunt Peggy's flawless Palmer-method penmanship. I marveled that his workman's hand showed such grace on the page.

By any contemporary measure, Uncle Buddy and Aunt Peggy were pretty unremarkable. He was a regular guy, a quiet working man. He provided modestly, but adequately, for his family. She was a kind, loving, good-hearted woman. She cared for everyone equally and seemed never to have anything unkind to say about anyone. After their deaths, the primary thing that could be said of them was that they were truly good people.

What did they do? By the world's measure, very little. Yet their lives were fulfilling, not only for themselves, but for many others around them. They added immeasurably to our family and to the world, not because of any particular deeds—though they did their share of kindnesses—but simply because of who they were.

Reflecting on the lives of Uncle Buddy and Aunt Peggy, and upon the lives of many others I have known, I am increasingly aware that what we do and what we have are of less importance than what we are. But all too often we define ourselves and measure our accomplishments and worth strictly in terms of what we own or possess. In the eyes of many, these signify success. Consequently, what we do becomes important for what it brings us in tangible goods or perceived power. Perhaps, for example, we are very well-off, or an authority in our field. But beyond these acquisitive drives, what does our doing and our being mean?

Everyone fashions and lives out some philosophy of life. Making sense of ourselves and our vocations is the primary work of our lives. In fact, what we do ultimately shapes our lives, like running water contours rock. If the meaning of my life is derived from possessing goods and power, then the means of achieving these goals may become the guiding philosophy of my life. Our tendencies toward workaholism suggest that many of us have lost any sense of our labor as a means of contributing to the common good and achieving personal satisfaction. Or that our appetite for more possessions or influence drives us to sacrifice our lives and our relationships to work. Or both.

There is some evidence that we are aware of the bankruptcy of these paths. Our hunger for worldly success is increasingly matched by a hunger for spiritual meaning. But we have not made peace between the two. We continue to pursue tangible goods and measurable power. But with equal intensity and conviction we pursue spiritual meaning, isolating this quest and attacking it much as we would a diet regimen or an exercise routine.

Yet, developing a meaningful philosophy of life, finding spiritual meaning in our life, is integral to who we are. It is also integral to what we do and have. By placing these dimensions of ourselves and our lives in conversation with one another our lives become whole, and integrated, and we become persons of integrity. It is only when we become persons of integrity that we can actually have a life.

What do you want to be when you grow up? That question has had as many answers as askings in the course of my own life. When I was very small, I probably responded as many children do: my answer reflected my latest fantasy or idolization. As I grew older, the fantasies began to spring from actual experience. For example, as I was learning to play the piano, I wondered what it might be like to be a concert artist, or to play with a pop orchestra, jazz ensemble, or rock band. When I realized I wasn't that good, I switched to organ lessons and, since I was good enough to play for services at my church, I began to think of church music as a possible career. My answer to what I wanted to be when I grew up began to reflect a connection with what I could actually do.

After seminary, I found myself managing a retail women's wear business. The job seemed an unlikely fit from the very beginning, but it served me well. It provided me time to clarify my vocation to priesthood. It gave me an opportunity and the means to live alone, on my own, and to experience the kind of personal growth that had been stunted by seven years of dormitory living in communities so small and so public they gave me renewed respect, and sympathy, for goldfish.

My time as a layman gave me new perspectives on the church and the workplace. The retail business taught me skills in financial management, public relations, and marketing that prove valuable every day in the evangelical and administrative tasks of ordained ministry. Long hours in six-day work weeks gave me new insights into the frustrations, griefs, and fears of the laity, and why traditional patterns of Sunday worship are often ill-suited to refresh an exhausted laborer. To many of my acquaintances and associates, those years are as silent and unknown as the hidden years of Jesus' life. Yet my person and my priesthood are indelibly stamped with the mark of those days: they have been a profound part of my present vocation and without them I would be diminished, and so would my ministry.

More importantly, however, the experience of managing a business taught me that to define myself and my life primarily in terms of my work was too limiting. I knew that whatever success I experienced as a retail manager was due, in part, to the ministerial skills others had recognized, encouraged, and nurtured on my way to and through seminary. But I was also to learn that whatever success I have enjoyed as a priest is due in part to the presence of administrative and managerial skills honed years back in retailing. And, at the deepest level, all of my accomplishments are the result of the gifts of life and ability given to me by God and my family.

When we lose sight and sense of how our lives relate, in any fulfilling way, to the larger world around us, we feel that our life has no meaning. If we are preoccupied with what we do and what we have, and these become the indices by which we value ourselves and others, we become cynical, apathetic, and individualistic—all expressions of despair. When confronted by the overwhelming demands of this world, demands that are pressed upon us every time we pick up a newspaper, open a magazine, tune in a radio, or turn on the television, we know that we can never do enough, we can never have enough.

When, however, we are attuned to our own gifts, interests, and abilities, and we are in conversation with our communities, we may begin to understand that what is asked of us, we have, and, when combined with the strengths of others, what we have is enough. This is the central premise behind the saying "Think globally, act locally." When the conversation is engaged, and we with it, we discover that the "call" is continual, and continually changing, to fit our needs, the world's needs, and, presumably, to fit God's will. This, I suspect, is how God comes to many of us. As we struggle to make meaning out of our lives, we find that meaning most clearly in those evidences that our lives are a genuine response to this "call." This is the heart of vocation.

The conversation may lead us to new tasks, even drastic changes in work and relationships. But for most of us, most of the time, the movements of the conversation are less dramatic; discerning and conforming to God's call does not always profoundly alter the substance of our lives. We may not be called to change what we *do*, but we shall certainly be called to reflect upon what we *are*.

I began with a reflection upon Uncle Buddy and Aunt Peggy, two people who are remembered by family and friends not for anything specific they did or had, but for what they were: they were good people. Along with Uncle Buddy and Aunt Peggy, we are all inheritors of a much older tradition. We are among the successive generations of believers who see within Jesus evidences not only of what we are to do, and what we might have, but of who and what we are. Jesus—or at least the story of Jesus—is part of our ongoing conversation. For some of us, Jesus is as much a partner in the conversation as any of our mentors and friends. But what Jesus has to contribute are not only his spoken words recorded in scripture, his verbal teachings and instruction. Equally important is what we discern from the unspoken—from examining and reflecting upon his life, his struggles and decisions.

In Jesus and through his experiences, we glimpse what it means to be in relationship with God. We see that relationship with God, as with any other person, is living and dynamic. Entering into and participating in such a commitment only initiates a conversation that lasts a lifetime. To live in relationship with another is to engage a deep conversation, one that will challenge us and change us. Who we are and what our being means depend, more than we appreciate, upon those with whom we relate along the way. Christians claim personal relationship with God in and through Jesus. We who invite his companionship also share his journey. I invite you into conversation with Jesus through an exploration of his own vocational discernment.

Guided by the Spirit, Simeon came into the temple; and when the parents brought in the child Jesus, to do for him what was customary under the law, Simeon took him in his arms and praised God, saying, "...my eyes have seen your salvation, which you have prepared in the presence of all peoples, a light for revelation...."

(Luke 2:27-32)

℈

2

The Weight of Expectation

I was named for my father. The choosing of my name, however, was not motivated by ego. It was prompted by crisis and fraught with fearful expectation. At the time of my birth my father lay critically ill in the hospital, recuperating from life-threatening surgery.

I am the firstborn of my family. It is quite possible that I might have been the only heritage of a marriage prematurely ended. Under the circumstances, I have long understood the legacy that was nearly mine to bear, if in name only. Fortunately, my father recovered and I share the legacy with four siblings—a much happier distribution of the load.

Still, nearly every time I sign my name and append "Jr." to it, I am aware that this name was chosen not so much in happy anticipation as out of anxiety. Such accidents of personal history, like their social and political counterparts, influence the shapes of our lives. I am who I am, in part, because of my parents' experiences—the events and emotions that attended my birth, determined my name, and formed our relationships with one another. To know this history is to better understand myself and my parents.

The path of vocational discernment leads backward as well as forward; to see where the path leads ahead, we need also to reflect upon all that lies behind. Imagining where we have come from, and who we have come from, helps us make sense of where and who we are now, and what we are to do. It helps us to make sense of our calling.

Admittedly, surrounded in my youth with many living relatives, I had little interest in those who were dead. I knew that on my father's side of the family, my ancestry consisted of hearty peasant stock whose roots could be traced to Sicily as recently as 1918. My mother's family had lived for generations in a rural region of North Carolina, a relatively uninteresting (to me) area of tobacco farms within easy distance of several modest-sized towns noted for textile, furniture, and tobacco manufacturing.

But, as a single young adult visiting with my family in North Carolina, a string of dismally rainy days propelled me to the local public library where I began scanning microfilm records of the earliest census of the area. Soon I was hooked on the detective work of genealogy. I spent hour after interesting hour searching out information. Before long, I was engrossed in a lively "conversation" with those who had gone before as I attempted to piece the fragments together, to learn what I could of those whose adventures and affections had made me who and what I am.

Eventually I learned that my maternal lineage could be traced to a small village in Switzerland in the earliest years of the Protestant Reformation. The parish register of the village church, one of the first congregations to abandon Roman Catholicism for the Reformed faith and practices, lists the name of the earliest member of our family. How did he arrive at this place, and why? No one knows for sure. Some believe that the hardship of famine and poverty brought him, as it moves so many, to a place where life could be sustained. But I have often wondered if, given his German name, he was moved to depart a Roman Catholic state for reasons of faith. His registration in the record of one of the oldest Reformed parishes situated due south of the German border seems more than a coincidence. And the deep religious convictions of succeeding generations only further confirm the suspicion that a hunger of the spirit, as much as any hunger in the belly, may have motivated his migration.

Of course at this distance, imagination must suffice for the lack of hard evidence. Much of any genealogical (or other historical) exploration depends upon it. In the case of my maternal ancestors, imagining that faith may have moved them helped me to see a parallel: my faith, like theirs, has literally moved me over borders—spiritual and geographical—I never dreamed of crossing.

When I began studying my paternal ancestry I found that access to information was hampered by their recent immigration to America, and by the differences between the meticulous record-keeping of Swiss Protestants and the haphazard notations of marginally literate Sicilian parish priests in remote villages. Still, the discovery of heraldic arms registered to several family names in my Sicilian line was sufficient to set my romantic imaginings into motion. From what houses and accomplishments did my relatives descend to the peasant stock I know? What fortunes, and tragedies, lead from my grandfather's labors in the coal mines of Pennsylvania and my cousin's hard labor as a shepherd on the scrubby hillsides of sun-baked Messina, back to gold lions rampant on a field of scarlet? There's a story there I long to know, but can only imagine.

Why did certain authors of the Christian gospels burden their narrative with lengthy and obscure genealogical lists tracing the ancestry of Jesus? In truth, these genealogies—like my own—contain more than a little romance. Yet even romance may serve us in our vocational quest: it nurtures our imagination. And imagining the lineage of Jesus is as much a part of the Christian's search for meaning as exploring our own family roots. We are invited, even commanded by scripture and tradition, to imagine ourselves members of God's household, brothers and sisters to Jesus himself. We are called to make this history our own and ponder its meaning in our own lives.

The gospel of Matthew probably begins with a lineage in order to impress upon its readers the royal pedigree of Jesus. Matthew traces the lineage of Jesus back to the heroic figure of Abraham, whose story marks the beginning of the formation of a people named Israel.

Luke, being more poetic and fanciful, is not content to stop with Abraham, but traces the lineage of Jesus all the way back to Adam. The genealogy of Luke's gospel is included to establish the priestly inheritance of Jesus by connecting him to that holy tradition.

Scholars assure us that neither of these genealogies is grounded in hard fact; indeed, it is difficult to know just how many of those persons named in the genealogies actually existed and how many were born of the human spirit's need to give mortal shape to eternal aspirations. To say that Jesus is descended of Adam, on one level, establishes Jesus as the heir of everything that we know to be human. To say that Jesus is descended of Abraham also suggests, on another level, that Jesus is heir of the human need for mythic heroes. It is probably wise to concede that both are true.

Like every family tree, the lineage of Jesus is certainly a mixed bag. In addition to those figures whose very existence may have been mythic, there are also some whose lives are rather well documented and manifest all shades of human experience. Named there are those who made great nations and lost them, those who were wise and those who were foolish, those who were upright and those who were low-down. But for our purposes, what these genealogies serve to tell us is that, like us, Jesus was born with a history.

Significantly, even the fanciful genealogies of Jesus found in the gospels are set within a historical frame that we can document. We are told that Herod was king in Judea and Augustus was emperor of Rome when Jesus was born. So while the genealogies remind us that Jesus was born with a history, their context reminds us that he was also born *into* history. At Jesus' birth, the convergence of his family history with the flow of human history establishes his particularity. His distinctiveness is marked by the fact of his parentage and the fact of his birth place and date.

These facts are important to us and to our vocation, too. Like Jesus, we are born with a history and situated in history. We are born of distinct genetic composition, the product of particular family trees. It is not for vanity alone that we contemplate our family history. To know thyself, as the philosopher has prescribed, is fundamental to one's life. To know oneself demands, at least in part, knowledge of one's history. Disconnected from our past, we do not know who we are.

Knowledge of our ancestors and their experiences helps us define who we are and how we are known in relationship to everything else around us. Therefore we see even in the life of Jesus how important the exercise of genealogical succession was. For those who sought to know who this person Jesus was and what bearing his life had on theirs it was important to know his history—or so the gospel writers thought. And if Jesus' experience was like our experience, this awareness was equally important for him, for it determined who he was.

In the context of Jesus' life, he was identified by the people he had been seen with and the families from which he was descended. These identities could be used both for blessing and for curse. Some knew Jesus as Joseph's son, and so marked his place in community. Those anxious to claim Jesus as heir to Israel's messianic prophecies identified him as David's descendant. Those who doubted or discredited him cited his relatively unimpressive parentage, Joseph the carpenter and Mary. We can be relatively sure that Jesus knew the power of each of these identities to limit or to open up possibilities—even as many of us know the power of such judgments as "Well, what more can be expected, she's just her mother's daughter," and "You do realize who his father was, don't you?"

Like Jesus, we are born into history, to a particular time and place, with no personal choice in the matter of our ancestry or our arrival. We arrive with certain limitations and are also born into the limitations of the era and the culture in which we live. Indeed, we are who we are by virtue of limitation.

Our bodies have shape, and our beings have personality; without these limits we would all have the shapeless physique of the amoeba and the personality to match. Drawing strict limits around light and concentrating its energies into a focused beam create the power of the laser, a power which allows something as insubstantial as light to cut through something as substantive as steel. Similarly, the insubstantial human soul is given power to act and serve in the gift of the human body; through its specific shape, the soul is given power to act and serve.

That this body is also limiting is painfully evident. When I asked a physician friend how I might improve upon a physique that is distinctly penguinesque, his simple reply was, "You should have picked your parents more wisely." Being descended from a long line of people built like eggplants certainly defines in part who I am and what I shall be able to do with my body. Some limitations are inherited.

Other limitations are inherent, determined by time. I was born in 1948 and might actually live to see 2020, give or take a decade: these dates also impose limits upon my life. I think I would have liked an opportunity to meet a Medici, especially as a cousin. I know I would have liked to have met Jesus—preferably with all my present knowledge of him—a long list of questions in hand, and ample opportunity to explore them. At the other end of the spectrum, I would love to think that I might live far enough into the future to see my dreams fulfilled. Who would not welcome long life if it promised the vision of a better world?

So, like Jesus, I am born with a history and born into history—these are accidents beyond my control.

I may lament this condition, but I cannot escape it. Yet in the life of Jesus I am reminded that while my vocation is defined in part by chronology, it is also empowered by *kairos*. *Kairos* is a Greek word sometimes rendered in the biblical phrase "the fullness of time." It is a particular time—the convergence of history and context, the making of moments. The birth of Jesus to a long line of historical people, into a specific moment in human history, has long defined for believers who Jesus is.

At the heart of our understanding of Jesus is this notion that his coming from whom, where, and when he did constitutes his particularity. Is not the same true of us? For us, as for Jesus, our sense of calling—discerning the meaning of our own lives—begins with who we are, where we are, and when we are.

And Jesus increased in wisdom and in years.
(Luke 2:52)

∂

3

Diving Into the Deep End

One of the greatest mysteries in the life of Jesus is the period between his birth and the commencement of his public ministry that begins with his baptism. Scripture is unspecific about the number of years that lapsed in between. Since those years are unaccounted for, we have no witness as to how they were spent. These "blank pages" in the story of Jesus have been sketched in various ways. And they have provided rich opportunity for the imaginative; many wonderful stories of how Jesus spent his childhood and young adult years can be found in the non-canonical writings of early Christianity and in drama and legend down to the present day.

Our popular characterizations of the adult Jesus have tended to portray him as introverted and meek. By extension, we have assumed that a similar meekness characterized him in the hidden years of his youth. However, the mythical stories of Jesus' hidden childhood often portray an arrogant little boy with obnoxious and spoiled characteristics, one who frequently plays tricks on his little friends—like turning stones into birds, and resurrecting playmates (after bumping them off, mind you).

It is little wonder that the gospels don't include such stories, but they do contain traces. Consider the uncharacteristically disrespectful, even snide, remark with which the boy Jesus greets his concerned parents who, upon realizing his absence, have doubled back in a frantic attempt to find him. Like a child interrupted in play with friends, Jesus meets a worried mother and father with an irritable, "Why were you searching for me?" (Luke 2:49). And the adult Jesus, just embarking on his ministry at a wedding in Cana of Galilee, is no less rude. When his mother observes that their late arrival has caused the wine to run out, Jesus disregards both his hosts and his mother with the retort, "Woman, what concern is that to you and to me?" (John 2:4). He sounds much like the teenaged or young adult male who seeks to break away from his mother's concern, but uses a blunt knife to sever the cord.

These references to Jesus' youthful impertinence in both the extra-canonical legends and in scripture suggest a truth about growing up: out of our worst and weakest features often come the resources of our greatest strengths. In fact, these characteristics of childhood and youth are often the manifestation of the very stuff of which self-confident leaders and mature sages are made. Time alone reveals and distinguishes the assured leaders from the insecure bullies.

The term "self-centered," then, can have two meanings. It can describe the despicable, selfish behavior of the young Jesus described above. But it can also point to the assured, grounded, and confident Jesus we encounter in his later life and ministry. Those who shaped the scriptural biographies of Jesus appreciated, and even discerned, that the occasional excesses or outbursts of youthful personality evidence the eventual strengths and virtues of mature leadership.

Common speculation suggests that Jesus was approximately thirty years of age when he presented himself to John the Baptizer at the Jordan River, although he may even have been as old as fifty. In either case, Jesus was somewhat older at his baptism than the age we normally associate with vocational decision. Indeed, given that life expectancies were probably shorter than our own, and that apprenticeships and marriages were undertaken earlier than is customary for us, even at thirty Jesus might have been considered "middle-aged" by his contemporaries when he began his work as an itinerant religious teacher. Regardless of his age, this was a big step and a frightening one.

When we read of Jesus' baptism—his decisive response to whatever compelling urge drew him to the water's edge—his experience and ours draw close. The story invites us to stand in this very place. Once there, we know again the mixture of fear and possibility, doubt and excitement that such moments provoke.

Beginning a new life is rather like diving into the deep end of a pool. It is simultaneously exciting and frightening. As a university chaplain, I live and work among young adults who are in the midst of these emotional waters. Some days excitement prevails; other days fear and anxiety are overwhelming. Most of the time, it is a swirling mixture of these emotions as we make our way through the many decisions that shape us. It is difficult to make a life, especially when there are so many choices.

But young adults are not the only folks splashing in the deep end of the pool these days. There are newly single people—divorced men and women, some who are single mothers and fathers—whose vocation to marriage has been challenged and changed. Once, they believed sincerely that they were called to a lifetime commitment to a particular partner, but that commitment has not held. There are unemployed women and men whose faith in corporate security has been challenged and changed. Once, they believed sincerely that they had found their life's work, and had secured their future well-being with their labor, but restructuring institutions and changing economic priorities have rendered them obsolete. There are the voluntarily unemployed, as well. They, too, once believed they had found their life's work, but subsequently determined that this work was no longer fulfilling or meaningful, or that it was incompatible with new priorities. And there are retired people who are challenged and changed: having expected and planned for an end, they find upon reaching it that they still have health, energy, and intellect to give beyond their own immediate need.

All of us share in common the deep end of the pool in these times of transition. We experience the exhilarating and scary possibilities that come of being in that place where the bottom is just beyond the reach of our toes. Some of us flounder and some float, some sink and some swim. But no matter how confident or competent we are, it is never prudent to swim unattended.

We learn that there are lifeguards and there are life guards. The former monitor our swimming for safety and rescue us from harm. They can be identified by uniforms—usually bright red or orange swimsuits. When they hear our exclamations of panic—"Help, help" and "Save me, I'm drowning!"—we know them by their swift response.

Life guards, on the other hand, guide and keep our feet in the paths defined by our limits. They can be identified by a uniform convention—the practice of identifying ourselves and each other in certain limited ways. We also know them through our responses in social interaction to the common question, "What do you do?" For after we say "hello," or exchange some other pleasantry, and share our names—with or without elaborations and digressions into family histories, geography, and social relationships—we inevitably come to "What do you do?" The answer to that question of vocation is my "life guard." It helps keep me on track.

At one point in my life my answer was that I was a corporate manager—more specifically, a general manager in a regional retail women's wear company. It wasn't just a job I did; I felt then, and in hindsight feel more strongly now, that I was called to be in that place and role. When I identify myself now as a priest, I define myself within a role. I can qualify that identity by adding that I am an Episcopal priest, thus situating my role within a particular communion. I can be more specific by adding that I am a university chaplain, or campus minister, and that I serve The University of Chicago, placing myself within a particular sphere of a community. Each of these identifiers serves as a guard around my life. Without them, I would lack specific identity or definition; my life would be amorphous.

Surely I am more than what I do. Yet I, and many others like me, persist in the notion that what I do is of such importance that it surpasses anything else one might know of me. That is why, until I could say with any confidence what I do, I was adrift and anxious in the world. That is also why, when I contemplate the loss of my position or experience boredom or dissatisfaction in my role, I become fearful and disoriented. Given the weight these matters have assumed in our lives, it is little wonder that some people are driven to despair for lack, or loss, of an answer to the question, "What do you do?"

Yet we have no idea what Jesus actually did for many—for most—of the years of his life. Some have tried to fill them in: many stories were recorded in the period when our scriptures were written, tales of how Jesus' youthful years were spent. But only one of them—Jesus' trip to the temple at age twelve and his precocious conversation with the learned elders—survives in the canon of scripture. Many more were discarded.

Were the missing years unimportant? Hardly. They were years of growth, to be sure. But what is primary to the gospels' introduction of Jesus is the moment when Jesus accepts full responsibility for his own life and vocation. That vocation is foreshadowed in the story of his adolescent visit to the temple where the boy engages the elders and amazes them with his facility in the scriptures—evidence that Jesus had obviously been studying for a long time. But this fleeting insight into his vocation is all we are given until Jesus shows up at the Jordan River's edge, there to be baptized by his cousin John.

At the very least, those of us who find ourselves still struggling with even basic questions of vocation can take some comfort in the possibility that Jesus was quite a mature adult when his vocation emerged with some clarity. We can appreciate that it took Jesus a good many years to discern this vocation and perhaps even more years to accept it for himself—and take this truth as a cue for our own lives. Moreover, we can surmise that the vocation for which we know Jesus was, perhaps, a second or even third vocation undertaken in the course of a life whose meaning was discerned not only in the most visible, recorded years, but in the silent and hidden ones as well. That should take some pressure off us. We see from the patterns of Jesus' life that vocation is "about time." To be called of God takes time, and to answer takes even more time.

The stories of Jesus tell us little about his sense of vocation, but they tell us much about the profound sense of purpose and meaning others derived from him. Those who recorded the story of their experience of Jesus were less interested in the facts of his life than they were in capturing how their experience of him had defined and affirmed their *own* lives. The first and only episode of his childhood to make the record is that strange meeting with the elders in the temple when he betrays an emerging sense of call in an enigmatic reference to being about his father's business— a reference which no one since has ever associated with carpentry.

But perhaps in those unrecorded years, Jesus was actually apprenticed to his father and studied carpentry. Maybe he worked with wood and earned a wage for his labors. This would certainly have made him a more compelling figure to those he called to share his ministry later on. Is it not more likely that they left their nets and their accounting tables to follow one who had obviously made a similar sacrifice?

The reality of those missing years of youth and young adulthood is that they have about as much relationship to Jesus' vocation as waiting tables has to do with the actor's artistry, or my work as a summer camp counselor, a dormitory advisor, or a retail manager has to do with my priesthood. That is to say they have everything to do with vocation.

Our experiences of learning and labor do shape who and what we are. Who I am and what I am cannot be separated from those experiences of childhood, youth, and young adulthood that defined the context of my living and shaped the contours of my life. Those opportunities frequently define where we are, in the most literal sense. We are often in a place because we desire to learn from certain teachers, or long to do a specific work, or simply because we need the money. In God's economy, nothing is wasted. Each of our experiences is important.

We cannot know how the young Jesus' learning and labor shaped him for his ultimate gift of ministry, but we can be sure that they did shape him. The actor waiting tables is learning valuable lessons that may later give special distinction to his dramatic art. Discipline, observation of human characteristics and behavior, attentiveness to service and detail, and collegiality in the ensemble that moves a meal from the chef's creative imagination, to the patron's desire, to the cook's stove, and back to the patron's table are but a few of the things the fledgling actor might learn in a restaurant.

The silence of those invisible years of Jesus' life tells us that while the work and learning of those years were important to his vocation, vocation is still distinct from work. That we confuse the two is evident in Jesus' ministry. We know that throughout his ministry there was a profound disjuncture between what the people expected and wanted him to do, and what he actually did. There was a distinct difference between their expectations and his vocation. This ought to be more apparent to us than it sometimes is.

The disparity becomes more apparent when we look at what we have of Jesus' life and realize how little we know of his work. We do not know what he did with his hands, how he was fed, whether he washed his own clothes or made his own bed, or where. All of these things, so important to our definition of self and so central to our understanding of who we are, are missing from our knowledge of Jesus. What is distinctive about our knowledge of Jesus' vocation is that it begins to be discernible in his baptism and the subsequent temptations he confronted.

The baptism of Jesus and the Christian rite of baptism are not synonymous. They are not even all that similar, unless we adhere to a strict practice of adult baptism—as some Christians obviously, and perhaps rightly, do. What the baptism of Jesus marks is more akin to our modern practice of confirmation: it is the moment when Jesus accepts full responsibility for his life. And that is when all hell literally breaks loose.

The gospel of Matthew says that God actually spoke on the occasion of Jesus' baptism: "This is my beloved Son, with whom I am well pleased" (Matthew 3:17). If God was pleased with anything in that event, surely it was in the assurance that at least one human being of all those created had finally assumed full responsibility for his own life and was thus ready for relationship. Since it is believed that God made human beings in order to have a loving, intimate relationship with them, it must have been one happy day in heaven when this finally began to look like it might really happen. After all, consider God's plight. Adam and Eve had been a profound disappointment. Abraham was promising, and with a certain amount of persuasion, Moses got as far as the mountain, a deep conversation, and a good smoke—if we count the fire atop Sinai. By the prophets' reckoning, Israel herself was a scandal, a fickle and unfaithful tease. Overall, God's relationships had been pretty unfulfilling.

Then came Jesus and suddenly God's hope was rekindled. As he stood in the waters of the Jordan, Jesus was not only sincere, he was mature. He was ready and able to commit. Ask anyone who has tried recently to find a person like that and you will know what a rare and happy occasion this was for God.

So among the first steps in Jesus' vocation was an act of radical personal commitment to another being—in this case, God. From this act we learn the profound connection between vocation and commitment to intimate relationship. We seldom consider the vocational nature of human relationships. Yet intimacy and our commitment to marriage, partnership, or celibate community are inherently vocational.

We do not achieve fulfillment in relationships by sheer force of will. That much should be obvious to anyone who has tried to will himself or herself into intimacy with another. We are *called* to relationship. We are called into intimate, committed relationship with other human beings—and with God. But we cannot respond to the call, or have such a relationship, until we are in possession of ourselves.

An important component of our growth into adulthood is the possibility of a new kind of relationship with our parents. Here we return to the traditional metaphors that suggest the father/son or parent/child paradigm as the model of the divine/human relationship. What brought pleasure to God at the time of Jesus' baptism was the self-possession that allowed Jesus to willingly choose an intimate commitment to God. In embracing responsibility for his own life, Jesus entered into a new relationship with God. Then, and perhaps only then, did they—and do we—fully realize what it means to love.

But Jesus learns that the willing acceptance of responsibility for one's life is not the end of it; it is only the beginning, as the wilderness experience proves. Because of his newfound responsibility, Jesus is tempted as soon as he has been baptized. It is terribly important to weigh the temptations in this balance of love—to see that what is really at stake and is truly being tempted is Jesus' power to choose. And the power of choice, like all power, is fraught with the capacity for good or for ill. Choice involves consequences that are not always evident, balances that can shift in an instant.

One summer at Boy Scout camp I had a lifesaving class that nearly killed me. At least it felt that way. The lifesaving class was conducted not in a pool, but in a small lake formed by a dam. The deepest point of the lake was at the dam. The instructor would hold up a galvanized peck bucket half-filled with hardened cement. He would then cast the bucket off the dam into the lake and each of us in turn would be required to dive to the bottom, recover the bucket, and bring it to the surface. In order to succeed, of course, we had to turn the bucket upside down, else the force of the lake water would hold it fast to the bottom.

My turn came and I watched as the bucket made an arc in the sky, hit the water, and disappeared. I moved into position and dived. The dark, muddy water made sighting the bucket impossible. But by groping I found it, upended it, and started my ascent. I reached the surface and raised the bucket to hand it off to the instructor. Before he could grab it, the bucket twisted on its handle. I was determined not to lose it. In the split second when I realized what was happening, I gulped a mouthful of air and, as I held tight to the bucket's handle, plunged like a rock to the bottom. Lungs aching and heart pounding, I wrestled the bucket back to the surface and finally handed it off to the instructor. I have never been able to use the expression "like tossing an anchor to a drowning man" without remembering that experience.

Each of the temptations possesses, for Jesus, the same potential as my bucket; each has the power to pull him beneath the waters and to drown him. First, Jesus is tempted to self-reliance. That is one way to understand why Satan invites him, a hungry man, to turn stones into bread. The temptations begin with egocentrism, a universal human trait. I don't know if Jesus could literally convert stones into bread; but I do know he could turn his convictions and his charismatic gifts to personal gain, a choice given to most of us. Instead, he counters this temptation with the affirmation that responsible exercise of self is found in interdependence: "One does not live by bread alone, but by every word that comes from the mouth of God" (Matthew 4:4). He was tempted to live by himself and to live only unto himself, reflecting the dark side of egocentrism. He chose instead to affirm that his life was not self-sustaining, but sustained in relationship with God.

Next the devil places Jesus on the pinnacle of the temple in Jerusalem. Hurl yourself down, says the tempter, "for it is written, 'He will command his angels concerning you,' and 'On their hands they will bear you up.'" Jesus readily identifies the real temptation when he replies, "Again it is written, 'Do not put the Lord your God to the test'" (Matthew 4:6-7).

Inherent in this temptation is the suggestion that Jesus should define his relationship with God on the basis of God's response to an independent action—like throwing himself off the temple. This is a singular test of Jesus' maturity and responsibility. For what Jesus is being offered here is the possibility of defining himself by the condition of the other's commitment to him. If you want to find out what your relationship to God really is, the tempter suggests, then see how God responds to you in time of need. What relationship has not known that temptation? Why settle for faith, when in the twinkling of an eye one can attain certain knowledge? Anyone who has ever been committed to another human being recognizes this temptation and occasionally succumbs to it.

Instead, Jesus determines that in his commitment to God it matters little how, or even if, God responds. Jesus' confidence in God is not to be tested, nor is Jesus' understanding of himself predicated upon what the other does—even if that other be God. Jesus will be who Jesus is, and will offer that in relationship to

God without regard to God's response. In this respect, Jesus definitely lives into his inheritance, for he demonstrates that he is very like the God who determined centuries before to love Israel, regardless of Israel's requital. Jesus reveals a security, a deep centeredness that allows him to give himself over to another without condition.

The tempter, however, is not easily rebuffed, and offers what he hopes will be the crowning blow: a temptation aimed at Jesus' confidence. For Jesus is obviously self-assured and of rare maturity, exhibiting tremendous human potency and potential. He possesses what many desire and seek in others—authority. And authority is the hallmark of any mature person who has accepted responsibility for his or her life. Satan seeks to undermine all of this by appealing to human vanity and venality, showing Jesus "all the kingdoms of the world and their splendor," and saying to him, "All these I will give you, if you will fall down and worship me" (Matthew 4:8-9).

Jesus was sorely tempted to accept the authority of celebrity that such splendid holdings would have secured for him. This was no vain offer—the tempter could easily have delivered. But Jesus would not have it, and Jesus did not want it. Jesus knew that true

authority and genuine leadership consist not in co-
opting the responsibility of others but in holding others responsible. He refused to buy the respect of others by shouldering their responsibility for them. Jesus
gave himself to others and literally encouraged
them—gave them the heart, the courage—to accept
responsibility for their own lives before God.

What Jesus experienced in the temptations is the
reality of responsibility—the perils and possibilities
that await us all. In the story of Jesus these are presented as temptations in one-time occurrences, if only
to illustrate the passage into vocation. But we can be
sure that the temptations are constantly there
throughout the vocational journey, as surely for us as
they were for Jesus. Indeed, we see glimpses of them
throughout his ministry—evidence that they do not
go quietly away and leave us alone.

Like Jesus, we are always and everywhere tempted
to live as though we are self-made, self-reliant crea-
tures. Jesus knew this temptation every time his words
or actions elicited the admiration or approval of others. We are constantly tempted to test the love of others, to *know* with certainty what we can only attain by
faith. But even Jesus was denied such knowledge; as
his own end approached his sweat was like drops of

blood, and he could not come down off the cross despite those who taunted him to do so. And we are forever tempted to see the world and its "kingdoms," its institutions, as our sovereign possessions, subject to our will. Jesus knew this well in the urgings of those who greeted his entry into Jerusalem with shouts. On the mount with Satan, or astride the donkey, the view was the same. And so was the temptation: take it all, make it all your own. These voices—and choices— never go away.

The temptations are of a single piece with the baptism itself and are always set in context with it in the gospels. They remind us that sheer determination does not fit us for vocation. Instead, the passage into the fullness of vocation is a gradual one, undertaken in conversation with a world that offers us many enticing, attractive alternatives.

Jesus emerges from the temptations with a sense of self-possession that can only be described as "self-centeredness." It is more than a confidence. It is a sense of assurance that reveals an essential trust of himself in relationship to his creator. He has cast off the support of whatever flotation devices buoyed him through his youth, and he has successfully resisted the temptations that surely would have destroyed him.

Thus it is quite plausible that the nasty legends of the child Jesus contain an element of truth: the self-centeredness of the youth might have been the foundation of that centered selfhood we know of the adult. We, too, may have gifts that we have undervalued or may even have sought to suppress in shame, resources essential to the full expression of our call. Gifts that await only their responsible exercise, in response to God's call, to find a divine purpose. Curses to be called into blessing.

He left Nazareth and made his home in
Capernaum by the sea, in the territory of
Zebulun and Naphtali...on the road by the
sea, across the Jordan, Galilee of the Gentiles.

(Matthew 4:13, 15)

℘
4

Crossing the Jordan

I n each of the gospels, the beginning of Jesus' public ministry varies. In Matthew's version, Jesus learns of his cousin John the Baptist's imprisonment and wisely leaves Nazareth to take up residence in Capernaum by Lake Galilee. One significance of the move is that it places Jesus on the opposite bank of the Jordan, in the region of the Gentiles.

Having crossed over, Jesus begins his ministry with a familiar proclamation: "Repent, for the kingdom of heaven has come near" (Matthew 4:17). It was the same message proclaimed by his cousin John. Was this coincidence an attempt to verify Jesus as John's successor? After all, John had built up an impressive following, many of whom resisted John's urgings to turn their attention and their faith to Jesus. Or could it be that Jesus entered his ministry a little less self-confident than we might have supposed, dependently following the footsteps of the one who had come before him?

I have suggested that Jesus emerged from the temptations with a new confidence and self-possession. But like ours, his progress into maturity was by no means instantaneous. And it was anything but neat and orderly. Like you or me, Jesus lived and moved among the conflicting forces of faith and doubt, confidence and crisis.

The early ministry of Jesus is marked by his teaching, and to a lesser extent, by healings and similar miraculous acts. There is more talk, more explicit conversation in those weeks of public, itinerant ministry; they are filled with parables and sermons. It is as though Jesus, like many of us, must "try on" his calling a little at a time, beginning with the relatively safe refuge of ideas. Indeed, with a few exceptions, Jesus seems to grow progressively more bold in his ministry as time passes. He moves beyond the obvious repetition of his cousin's message, venturing little by little into his own territory. Only gradually does he move from notion to action until, little by little, his work becomes truly incarnate, embodied in physical acts.

One common element in the gospel narratives is the story of Jesus' call of the disciples. By the sea of Galilee he meets and calls brothers Simon Peter and Andrew, fishermen who are invited to ply their skills in new ways and new "waters." Passing a tax booth, he greets Matthew, also called Levi, and invites him to follow. On one level it might seem to us that Jesus is organizing a campaign or setting up shop. Perhaps this is because we view the stories through what is familiar in our day; we read backward through the lens of institutional and church history and see in these early associations the pattern of our own administrative structures. But is it not curious that when Jesus calls these early companions, he is terribly hazy about job descriptions and mission statements?

Clearly, the pattern here is somewhat different. The relationship between Jesus and his disciples emerges as more that of friends than of professional staff. There is no evidence of how he comes to choose the particular individuals he chooses. No rationale is offered and no apparent design for their deployment emerges. He is not hiring workers or associates, but calling friends.

In one sense, Jesus' experience is familiar. We, too, tend to embrace friends more readily in those early years away from home. For many of us this is the first opportunity to make friends of strangers, to make friends we can truly call our own.

Many of our childhood friendships are controlled by ties of kinship or managed subtly, but managed nonetheless, by family and parental opinions and relationships. Decisions like where we shall live when we are children, and where we shall go to school, are agonizing for our parents. Families uproot and move lock, stock, and barrel to avoid the potential or implied threat of unsavory friendships and questionable classroom influences that might shape our lives for ill.

Moving to the other side of our own Jordan is a move that takes us beyond such control and its constraints. Gentiles are different—and that difference makes them exotic. The taste of freedom and autonomy that we associate with the other side of the river, the compelling newness of everything we find there, are exciting for many of us. Mark Twain understood the attraction of the foreign, which is often the forbidden. He maintained that God made a tremendous misjudgment of human nature in Eden. God ought not to have forbidden Adam and Eve to eat the apple;

God should have commanded them not to eat the snake.

Jesus' selection of his own circle of companions may well have been something more than a conscious organizational plan for the implementation of a well-planned ministry. It may have been his first opportunity to choose friends freely. Like Jesus, when we are free from the familial and the familiar and offered the opportunity of new circumstances, we find and embrace those friends who are of our own choosing. They are uniquely ours, and in that uniqueness lies much of their preciousness. In these relationships we often share everything. Most importantly, through them we build sufficient confidence in others to express our ideas openly.

As a youth and young adult, I did not find home the most compatible or comfortable place to let my ideas range, free and untethered. I never realized ideas could be so volatile until I slipped and let a few of them roll out in front of my parents and siblings. Even among some of my friends at school, I was cautious in what I shared. My whole social order—which, of course, was the very order that held my universe in place—could come unglued if I was not discrete.

It was only among a few select friends—nearly every one of whom my parents disapproved—that I dared to share my ideas. High school confidantes joined in the conspiracy and we supported one another, but we were still under the watchful eye of teachers and parents, family and friends whose very presence was a reminder of our confining restraint.

It was at the University of North Carolina in a place called Chapel Hill, on the other side of the Jordan where the gentiles lived and partied, that I found safe harbor for that fleet navigating my imagination. There I met and was befriended, even beloved, by strangers—many of them fellow escapees. We shared the forbidden joys of cold beer, endless cigarettes, and long evenings of playful conversation. And we forged a love that in some cases has lasted throughout our lives.

While the ideas and dreams we share among youthful friends remain important to some of us for a lifetime, there is something special about those whose potency raises them to the status of ideals—those thoughts that are simply outrageous and consequently open us to possibilities beyond our learned constraints. In the company of friends the effect of this exploration is magnified, and we draw encouragement from one another to dare.

In its negative form, this dynamic makes the street gang a potent and dangerous force in both the lives of its members and in the community it assaults. But in its positive manifestation, exploration of this kind feeds the imagination, which is the heart of human being and the soul of faith.

Something else rather remarkable happens relative to Jesus' relationships in the period of his early public ministry: he redefines his family. It is a radical move, appearing somewhat early in Mark's account, later in Matthew and Luke. Jesus is gathered with a sizable group, apparently in someone's house. His mother is outside, along with his brothers and sisters. In Mark's account:

> They sent to him and called him. A crowd was sitting about him; and they said to him, "Your mother and your brothers and sisters are outside, asking for you." And he replied, "Who are my mother and my brothers?" And looking at those who sat around him, he said, "Here are my mother and my brothers! Whoever does the will of God is my brother and sister and mother." (Mark 3:31-35)

This new perspective on relationship is only one step, but a very significant one, in the progression that Jesus makes from the wilderness into the company of the disciples, from Nazareth to Galilee, and from kin to community. There is much to be learned from attention to the maturation of Jesus.

If, as our creeds maintain, Jesus was "fully human," then merely to focus upon his recorded words and deeds—important as they are—is still to overlook the very substance of his life. It is his life that is given to us, and that gift can be helpful in our own discernment process. John's gospel maintains that Jesus' gift to us is that we might have life in all its fullness. God's call, the source of our vocation, is a call to life's fullness along a pathway charted by Jesus.

That pathway, as we see from his own life, led Jesus from the security of home and family into the lonely struggle of the wilderness temptations. It brought him into the company of chosen companions. It literally took him from the safe boundaries of his hometown to the opposite side of the very river that secured his homeland from the land of the Gentile stranger. In that unusual exchange where Jesus seems to reject his own family, the path veers away from the primary unit of association and opens Jesus to embrace in trust the circle beyond his own blood.

This point may be particularly important to us in today's culture, where so many dimensions of our own vocational quest touch upon family relationships. Breaking away from our dependencies upon those relationships and moving beyond their deficiencies are difficult but essential pieces of the vocational process. For vocation includes the totality of our life.

Vocation includes not only our call to work, but our call to love as well. The church has long taught that marriage is not simply an act of will or a social convention, but a response to God's call to enter into intimate covenant with another. By extension, those not called to marriage are in no way deemed inferior in the eyes of the church or in the eyes of God. They are rather called and equipped by God to invest their love in other ways, the most prominent in our tradition being celibate vocation. Today we as a community seek wisdom and discernment as we attempt to know of God whether and how God's call might lead to still greater diversity of relationship. This is the real issue at the heart of our wrestling with sexuality. Matters of human intimacy and sexuality are as much a part of our vocational quest as our desire to find our life's work.

What we observe in Jesus' pilgrimage of vocational fulfillment is that he experienced a series of radical changes and reorientations. Each one was essential to his formation as a person, and each was a response to vocational urging. That he found himself knee-deep in the Jordan being baptized by John, or living in Galilee on the opposing bank of the Jordan from Nazareth, or in the midst of strange but chosen companions, or broadening his notion of family to include those who were not tied to him by blood or nationality, was not by whimsy or will. He was where he was and what he was in response to his discernment of God's will for him, God's call to him.

Thus we ought not be surprised in our own journey that similar demands might be made of us, that the promptings of God might urge us into what can only be deemed difficulty. For to admit the reality of God's place in our lives and to assent to relationship with God as Jesus did at his baptism, and as we all do through our baptisms, is difficult—especially for self-sufficient human beings. To leave home and take up residence either literally or ideologically on the opposite bank from where we originated is difficult. To cast off the protective shelter of the familiar and predictable and take up with strangers is difficult. To respect but renegotiate one's relationship to one's family is painfully difficult.

What the gospels reveal to us in the less obvious dimensions of Jesus' vocation is most assuredly "good news." To see that the path of God undertaken by Jesus looks more than vaguely familiar, congruent with our own experiences, is to be reassured in our own shaky steps. But there is one more detail of this early ministry that can both compel and comfort.

We seem to assume that in matters of vocational discernment Jesus was blessed with an eerie self-confidence that is denied us. The Jesus of the gospels is annoyingly sure of himself. But hidden in the corners of the story are slight evidences that not all Jesus' humanity was edited out of the stories of the early church. The reality of Jesus' experience of our own failings and frailties survives, if only in fragments.

One such snippet is found in Mark's account of the healing of a blind man at Bethsaida. The blind man has been brought to Jesus by friends who beg Jesus to touch the man and restore his sight. But Jesus takes the man by the hand and leads him out of the village. Perhaps Jesus withdrew because he was intent upon determining whether sight was truly what the blind man desired, for nowhere in the story does it say that the man himself actually requested to be healed. We also know that it is often characteristic of Mark's gospel to show Jesus working his miracles in private and, as in this instance, warning the healed person not to say anything publicly about his or her miraculous cure.

Evidently Mark was struggling with a legitimate question: how could Jesus have done so much among so many and still not have been accepted for the truth of what he was? Perhaps Mark surmised that Jesus intentionally obscured the reality of his being from them. But there are other intriguing suggestions in the wonderfully funny exchange between Jesus and the man from Bethsaida.

Jesus spits on the man's eyes and then covers them with his hand. In these maneuvers Jesus is following a rather common ritual practice. But when Jesus removes his hands, there is no confidence. "Can you see anything?" Jesus asks the man (Mark 8:23). Recall that elsewhere Jesus is reported to have cured people in absentia, that without even touching a man's deceased child, he merely tells the man to go home and he will find his daughter well. There is no such confidence here. Off by themselves, Jesus and the blind man from Bethsaida are struggling to get it right.

The blind man does not appear to have been born blind. He reveals in his answer that he knows the difference between people and trees when he says to Jesus, through his squint, "I can see people, but they look like trees, walking" (Mark 8:24). So Jesus tries a second time, placing his hands on the man's eyes, and the man's sight is restored.

This casual but significant detail points to the progressive, and sometimes halting, journey toward vocational fulfillment. It reveals to us that Jesus didn't always get it exactly right the first time, every time— that he probably had moments of self-doubt and even ineptitude. When we try to convince ourselves that Jesus was perfect, we rob him of his fullness. We dispute the truth that he was in every way as we are. Moreover, the complete text is: "he was in every way as we are, yet did not sin." In denying Jesus' failures, we confuse and deny an essential and fundamental truth. We equate failure with sin, and that is heresy.

Perhaps more than any other, that heresy threatens to harm our relationship with God in Jesus, and thus impede vocation. It is most evident and poses particular risk in our high, and often unattainable, standards of perfection. The conflict between impossible expectations of human perfection and our unsuccessful quest to attain them can lead to spiritual anorexia—a literal loss of appetite for living.

In many respects Jesus seems to have failed in his life. He failed to fulfill his community's expectations that he would settle in Nazareth and contribute to the economy, both in his work and in the making and nurturing of a family. He must have failed political and tribal expectations when he took up residence on the opposing bank of the Jordan in Galilee, in the land of the Gentiles. He no doubt disappointed his childhood friends when he left them and took up with a new crowd of his own choosing. And how could he not have hurt his mother, his brothers, and his sisters in that moment when he refused to go out to them, and even denied them their primary claim upon his affection by supplanting them with those strangers? Moment by moment and step by step, Jesus' vocation—at least from varied perspectives—must have seemed a colossal failure.

That he did not and could not fulfill everyone's notion of perfection, that his own confidence in himself was not rock-solid, that he was somewhat tentative and shy in that less than stunning exhibition of healing in Bethsaida reveal a person whose vocation bears more than faint resemblance to my own experience. Thinking upon these things, my love and admiration for Jesus only grow.

But Jesus also frightens me. By including strangers into the intimate circle called family, and in his subsequent instructions to his disciples to travel with a single bag, accept the hospitality of unknowns, and eat what is offered, he challenges all the customary boundaries that define us. His patterns of dining, which took him from table to table and completely traversed the social order of his day, are for Jesus the reality of the kingdom. His is a table without the arbitrary boundaries we erect, a table where hospitality prevails.

In his open healing, Jesus crosses the boundaries of touch. Jesus touched over and over again—he violated quarantine. I think again of my first friendships away at college among the gentiles. We were initially strangers, from different social classes and races. But then we found ourselves at table, eating and drinking. We, too, were crossing our own boundaries, maybe not on any magnificent scale—but then one could argue that Galilee was hardly the center of the universe. Nonetheless, the boundaries Jesus crossed had great and lasting significance for his vocation.

I admit that I still find it difficult to breach the boundaries, to venture what I risked at tables shared in those first years among the gentiles, on the wilder side of my Jordan. But my vocation—my being where I am—is linked in some crucial way to those experiences. Through them I experienced the inbreaking and indwelling of the holy. Perhaps that is at least one function of the eucharistic table: to practice regularly the intentional violation of the customary boundaries that separate us and, in the vulnerable act of a meal shared with strangers, experience the intimacy of spiritual communion. The way to God is through all that separates me from those earlier experiences among the first gentiles I met, when I could still taste the Jordan in my mouth, and shudder with the pleasure of having made the crossing.

Jesus took with him Peter and James and John, and led them up a high mountain apart, by themselves. And he was transfigured before them, and his clothes became dazzling white, such as no one on earth could bleach them. And there appeared to them Elijah with Moses, who were talking with Jesus. Then Peter said to Jesus, "Rabbi, it is good for us to be here; let us make three dwellings, one for you, one for Moses, and one for Elijah." He did not know what to say, for they were terrified. Then a cloud overshadowed them, and from the cloud there came a voice, "This is my Son, my Beloved; listen to him!" Suddenly when they looked around, they saw no one with them any more, but only Jesus.

(Mark 9:2-8)

℘
5

Out in the Open

In each version of the transfiguration story as told in Matthew, Mark, and Luke, Jesus begins by ruminating openly upon his impending suffering and death: "He began to teach them that the Son of Man must undergo great suffering, and be rejected by the elders, the chief priests, and the scribes, and be killed, and after three days rise again. He said all this quite openly" (Mark 8:31-32). There is a purpose in such a juxtaposition. But that purpose is not apparent until we consider these events from a vocational perspective.

There can be no doubt that something significant happens in the life of a person who confronts personal mortality. We tend to trivialize this important event with glib references to "mid-life crisis." But Jesus was very frank in his meditations upon mortality; scripture insists that he shared his intimations "quite openly." Have we even begun to fathom what he was talking about?

I do not believe that Jesus somehow saw his future as different in any way from yours and mine. I do believe, however, that there came a time in his life—as comes to most of us—when Jesus was acutely aware of the cost of seeing his call to completion, and painfully aware of the death that concludes this mortal journey. Such an awareness has a very sobering effect upon a person. And these insights into truth strike a note of fear as well.

At this point in his life, Jesus knew where his path was leading him. At first he had confined himself to rather commonplace teaching, such as the pithy, proverbial wisdom sayings gathered up in the Sermon on the Mount. Then he became more widely known for his healing work among the people. Still, there was nothing terribly extraordinary about these achievements. Hills and alleys were full of figures much like Jesus, each with his or her own following. Or *was* there something different about him?

When Jesus first began his work of preaching, teaching, and healing, he resorted most often to parable and its poetics, cloaking his message from all save those who actually listened thoughtfully and critically. He told stories of farmers whose seed fell in different soils and suffered varied ends; he likened the life God desired for us to a rare pearl, an abundant catch of fish, and a mustard seed.

But when Jesus moved beyond parable to outright critique and condemnation of those in power, even people who had only half-heard the parables sat up and took notice. He tossed all politeness and poetry aside and openly denounced injustice, wrongdoing, and religious malpractice. The healings of Jesus—particularly the one involving a man whose withered hand was restored by Jesus on the Sabbath—became all the more remarkable as they broke through the boundaries of ritual purity law and just plain common sense. Indeed, these acts became subversive.

As the people responded more enthusiastically to such naked truth, Jesus drew more attention to himself. After a point, this attention elicited the interest, then the concern and examination, of the Pharisees—those who ruled over church and political affairs and were, in short, the makers and keepers of the boundaries.

It was no secret that the dominant religious parties—Pharisee and Sadducee—were growing intolerant of Jesus' denunciations. Nor was Herod amused by anyone who disturbed the peace and order of his territories. While he may have had little interest in the theological dimensions of Jesus' teaching, any unrest, regardless of the cause or the source, reflected badly upon Herod's abilities to maintain order and endangered his standing with the imperial court in Rome. After all, his job was to maintain the empire's political and social boundaries.

The reality was plainly evident: Jesus moved irresistibly toward trouble. Every time he opened his mouth, he could not help himself. He moved steadily into danger with his frank appraisal of the state of affairs around him. His reflections upon mortality were not the product of despair—they were simply an honest appraisal of where things were headed. Only genuine friends can tolerate such honesty. Evidently, he had a few friends, even among those he denounced.

Luke's gospel indicates that it was some Pharisees who came to Jesus and warned him to get out of

Jerusalem, assuring him that Herod did want to have him executed. This detail suggests that Jesus had been assisted all along by those within the institutions of his culture who shared his desire for reform. No doubt they had defended him many times, both in temple and at court.

The Johannine gospel actually names Nicodemus, a Pharisee who took the time and care to discuss theology with Jesus: "He came to Jesus by night and said to him, 'Rabbi, we know that you are a teacher who has come from God; for no one can do these signs that you do apart from the presence of God'" (John 3:2). As Jesus' activities—and reports of them—provoked the Pharisees, and hostility toward him escalated, Nicodemus and perhaps others like him may have interceded for Jesus in the councils of religious leadership. Counseling prudence, Nicodemus asks of his Pharisaical colleagues, "Our law does not judge people without first giving them a hearing to find out what they are doing, does it?" But the retort, "Surely you are not also from Galilee, are you?" silences Nicodemus, for it implies that any ally of Jesus can expect to share his fate (John 7: 51-2). After a point, none of the arguments from those sympathetic to Jesus could prevail over the majority power.

In adhering to his own vocation, Jesus made it difficult for those who wished to help. Ultimately, their paths separated from his. They parted ways when Jesus exceeded their boundaries, when he surpassed their understanding. Jesus could see the necessity of parting and realized that, in truth, while vocation is certainly social, vocation is also intensely singular.

As Jesus confronted the reality of his call, he knew it included his dying—but not in any melodramatic sense. After all, to see Jesus' open ruminations upon his death as mystical forebodings or foreshadowings inserted into the gospel narratives—like *sotto voce* secrets delivered by an actor to his audience—is to make him somewhat psychic and removed from our own experience. Nor were Jesus' reflections upon death merely political realism. That would make Jesus the agent of his own execution: he stirred up trouble, he was asking for it. He knew his enemies were gunning for him and provoked it.

No, Jesus' comments on death may have been nothing more than the open expression of his comfort with the truth of his own mortality. That alone distinguishes him even as it universalizes him. An essential component of vocation is this personal appropriation of the truth of our own end, and a willingness to openly embrace it in our public life.

This is not fatalistic, nor is it suicidal. It is simply truthful. No one in Jesus' company wanted to hear of such realities, and we know they protested when he brought them up. But when they persisted in not hearing, when they proved incapable of actually supporting Jesus with their love and friendship but rather encouraged a wholesale denial of truth, Jesus lost it. On one such occasion he labeled Peter the incarnation of Satan himself. On all such occasions tensions were palpable. This is always the case when boundaries that are in place are challenged.

But it was particularly on these occasions that Jesus invited companionship. "If any want to become my followers, let them deny themselves and take up their cross and follow me" (Matthew 16:24). This is perhaps the clearest invitation to discipleship in all of Christian scripture. Extending beyond the close circle of twelve, this general invitation includes all of us. At this moment in Jesus' life our vocation and his intersect in a special way. For that reason, it becomes all the more important that we examine it with care.

Why did he not make this invitation earlier? It is not part of those vast scenes when there were huge

multitudes around. It does not accompany his healings or his miracles. It does not come in any of those
instances when those gathered near to him would
have been most likely to respond affirmatively. At no
other time was he so forthcoming. Only now, at the
moment of his own reckoning with mortality and the
singularity of his life, does Jesus issue the invitation.
And this points to a radical reality.

For, indeed, Jesus invites us into a radical reality.
This is the crucial parting of the ways. It was for him
and it remains so for us in our generation and our culture. What those around Jesus resisted was the call to
live into the reality of mortality. What Jesus determined to do on this occasion was to embrace the mortality at the heart of every human vocation.

Jesus invites us, too, to cross the boundary we
have erected against this truth. He invites us to enter
into the openness of a life that imposes no boundaries
between living and dying. But we are not so quick to
follow. For us, death is an enemy. We fortify our lives
against it. We deny it. We bargain with it. We attempt
in every way we can to circumvent it. Some of us
spend a lifetime running from the inevitability that
awaits every human life, never once considering that
this universal experience is itself a part of our voca-

tion to be human. In calling us into being, in calling us into birth, in calling us into life, God also calls us into death. This is what Jesus surely recognized, and into this vocation Jesus determined to live.

Jesus did not, however, adopt the attitude of a fatalist, though that is always a choice given and an option sometimes taken. Neither did Jesus submit or resign himself to death. He submitted to an open life which, in turn, made him vulnerable and accessible to human will. Death was merely the instrument of human social, religious, and political entities, delivered in the foolish belief that death really is a boundary that can separate us. Those who killed Jesus had no investment in his death; it was an impersonal, institutional act. For them, death and a sealed tomb were but one more way to clearly and definitively demarcate the boundary that separated them from Jesus and his truth.

Jesus was truly reconciled with death, even as St. Francis of Assisi embraced death as a sister. Jesus did what every true peacemaker does: he made friends with the enemy. Ponder this notion when considering the last of the beatitudes, the one that blesses the peacemaker and recognizes the peacemaker as the son and daughter of God.

Jesus made family of the enemy even as he had earlier made family of strangers. He looked across the boundaries and saw death not as something to be denied or defeated, but embraced. He reached across, stepped across the boundaries, and embraced death as a companion on the way. Being thus reconciled, all those energies of the human spirit that one might give to resistance were immediately accessible for offering as a gift to God.

About a week after speaking of his own death and inviting others into an open life, says Luke's account, Jesus withdrew with Peter and James to pray. While he was in prayer, his appearance changed. It was perceived that Moses and Elijah stood to either side of him and talked with him.

The appearance of these figures is not nearly as interesting as Luke's statement that they actually talked with Jesus. Could it have been that through this poetic vision and conversation Jesus made peace with his own history and found affirmation of his true vocation? The image of Jesus in conversation with the patriarchs becomes, then, a reunion of sorts. It is a momentary reaffirmation of Jesus' baptism and, seen in this light, bears much in common with that earlier event. For after this transfiguring experience, Jesus left Galilee and began the journey to Jerusalem.

The decision to go to Jerusalem was yet another crossing of boundaries. Herod had drawn a line in the sand. The religious officials had done the same. Jesus' determination to return to Jerusalem was a breeching of both prohibitions.

But there were other boundaries, too. There were all the bonds of society that connected Jesus to those around him. He could capitulate to the demands of his friends and supporters; he could remain safe with them and within their bounds. He could remain forever in Nazareth, tending the shop and caring for his immediate family. He could conform to political wisdom and common expectation and thus save his life. But to have done so would have been a death of a different kind: the stifling of a life and the denial of a call.

When he came down from the mountain, Jesus resolved to do as Abraham before him had done: he would take that step toward God that is at one and the same time the first and the final step of vocation. He would go to Jerusalem. He would step into the unknown.

There was no way of knowing precisely what would happen. This was a step out of the safety and the security of control. It was a step away from the comforting confines of others' opinions, away from the advisory admonishments and political protections of others and even beyond Jesus' own best judgments. It was a step that would render him alone, set into a solitary way. This decision and its consequences were uniquely his.

And yet, through his decision there is a universal opening: from this very place Jesus issues each of us an invitation to follow. Our following will take us down a different path. While Jesus' path leads to death on a cross, he assures us that each of our "crosses" will be different—no less challenging or difficult, perhaps, but certainly different, unique. Contemplating this experience, Annie Dillard asks:

> Why do you never find anything written about that idiosyncratic thought you advert to, about your fascination with something no one else understands? Because it is up to you. There is something you find interesting, for a reason hard to explain. It is hard to explain because you have never read it on any page; there you

begin. You were made and set here to give voice to this, your own astonishment.[1]

Each of us ultimately arrives at that solitary place where decision and consequence are uniquely ours, a point that is both end and beginning. But others have stood in this place; Jesus has stood here. With him, we are alone, together.

Endnotes

1. Annie Dillard, *The Writing Life* (New York: Harper & Row, 1989), 67-68.

When they came from Bethany, he was hungry. Seeing in the distance a fig tree in leaf, he went to see whether perhaps he would find anything on it. When he came to it, he found nothing but leaves, for it was not the season for figs. He said to it, "May no one ever eat fruit from you again." And his disciples heard it.

(Mark 11:12-14)

Jesus was a Cross Maker

On one matter, the several records of Jesus' last week in Jerusalem are consistent. From the moment he enters the city, everything runs out of control. Whatever else that mysterious fig tree may mean, it seems a poignant detail confirming the suspicion that sometimes even nature conspires against us—winter snow foils, spring rain frustrates, summer heat fries—and nothing is going our way. What does it matter that Jesus is hungry? It is not the season for figs.

At least one sector of the population greets his entrance into Jerusalem with near hysterical abandon, literally paving his path with the clothes off their backs in token of their support for him, and with branches of palm that were normally reserved for military victory.

Jesus shows up in the temple, the very precincts of danger itself. There he plainly throws a fit, losing his temper and flinging furniture and epithets with an uncharacteristic vehemence:

> Jesus entered the temple and drove out all who were selling and buying...and he overturned the tables of the money changers and the seats of those who sold doves. He said to them, "It is written, 'My house shall be called a house of prayer'; but you are making it a den of robbers." (Matthew 21:12-13)

Jesus seems unbounded. He is perhaps no less centered, but he is plainly no longer self-possessed. Even though the tales of childhood pranks and outright wickedness attributed to Jesus in legend and extra-canonical literature were omitted from the scriptures we now study, one strange episode of unseemly and spiteful adult anger survives. In the only instance of genuine malevolence recorded of him in our canon, Jesus curses a fig tree because it bears no fruit, despite the fact that it is not the season for figs. Reportedly, the tree dies. Even as allegory, this is a bitter story.

Not surprisingly, as Jesus grows more prominent, questions about his authority are raised. Jesus replies to those questions rather tersely or not at all. Such parables as he tells are more pointed and their lessons less opaque. He specifically denounces the teachers of the law and he dares to speak of the destruction of the temple itself. Jesus alludes to plots and secret plans, urging his disciples to watchfulness—perhaps as much to remind himself as anyone else. In Bethany he is anointed with costly perfumed oils, an act which proves to be the last straw for the most zealous of his closest followers. Then Judas, acting on personal convictions, takes his own step, uniting himself with those who seek to put Jesus away.

By the time Jesus sits at table with his friends and disciples in that room apart, everything is in chaos. Up to the final entry into Jerusalem, while things had gone back and forth and up and down, there had been a balance and order to their lives. There had been setbacks, and they could also measure tangible progress. But from the moment they enter Jerusalem, there is a palpable difference. Jesus seems oddly distant, or at best, distracted. He relates to those around him quite differently than in the earlier months they had shared: he seems more aloof. On the night of his arrest, at the table with them, the breakdown is so pronounced that words fail to serve.

Jesus realizes that the disciples do not understand what the evening is about. They argue about preference and status. Jesus grows more and more silent even as they grow more and more animated, fascinated with his tumultuous reception in Jerusalem, and his sudden change in demeanor. Maybe his disciples are accustomed to arbitrariness, whim, and arrogance as the standards of leadership. Maybe they dismiss his new moodiness as evidence of an emerging political rebel. Perhaps in their eyes he is finally taking on the characteristics of the leader they desire him to be.

As the disciples grow enlivened with wine and excited by visions of revolutionary reform, they are hardly aware of his silence until they are startled to find him washing their feet. Peter attempts to make light of it, and even ventures a joke by offering to let Jesus give him a whole bath. But the tension is palpable. Even their wine cannot take the edge off it.

The disciples are probably relieved when he suggests that they withdraw for prayer. This was often an invitation to huddle for special counsel with him. But they are very sleepy, and Jesus is acting very strangely. So they let him pray and make the motions of keeping watch. They are oblivious to any real danger and consequently they nod off.

The ordeal of prayer in Gethsemane is portrayed as the loneliest moment in Jesus' final days. Artists good and bad alike have portrayed the figure of Jesus, his eyes lifted to an unanswering sky, his brow anguished and drenched with sweat, his hands locked in that way we instinctively entwine our fingers when they are shaking out of control.

But the truth of the matter is that from the time Jesus emerges from the experience of the transfiguration and sets his feet toward Jerusalem, he is alone. He may be surrounded by people, even warmly embraced by them, but so much about the record tells, in detail after revealing detail, that Jesus is painfully, horribly alone.

On so many other occasions in times of crisis, the story describes angelic intervention, or heavenly voices, or descending doves—some evidence of God's presence and attention. But from the moment Jesus emerges from the experience of the transfiguration until the very end of his life, there is no evidence whatsoever of any response to his anguish.

In earlier days he was known for his ease in touching others—placing his hands on the sick, taking children into his arms, embracing his friends. Now, with the exception of the footwashing, it is not he who touches, but who is touched. The crowd struggles to touch him as he enters Jerusalem's gate. A woman lavishes him with expensive oil at supper in Bethany. A beloved disciple lays his head upon Jesus' breast at the supper table. Soldiers lay hands upon him in the garden, and lashes upon him in his imprisonment.

The angry crowd begs to have him released into their hands instead of a criminal named Barabbas. Veronica is said to have stepped out of the spectators to wipe the sweat from his face as he climbed toward the place of execution. Dutiful henchmen hold him to the wood and impale him upon it, then touch his lips with vinegared wine and lance his side with the spear. His body is lowered into waiting hands and arms, anointed with experienced palms and fingers that work the embalming ointments into his lifeless skin. And after he is resurrected, all his friends want to do is touch him.

Touch is control. So long as it is our hand that makes the first move, our will that connects flesh to flesh, it is we who are in control. If we feel uneasy or threatened, we cringe from being touched; we recoil from the thought of it. My own reflexes are extremely sensitive to touch. I am unbearably ticklish. This ticklishness is evidence of my own tension at being caught out of control. In that last week of Jesus' life in Jerusalem everything was out of control, including Jesus himself. Can there be any bolder symbol of resignation than to submit to the touch of others?

What we are privileged to witness through the stories of the gospel writers is the struggle of Jesus as he gradually makes his way into the fullness of his own vocation and finally surrenders to it. We share Jesus' perspective as he faces into his vocation. In the final days of that last week, we witness his struggle to give over his life. Annie Dillard writes of this vocation:

> One of the few things I know about writing is this: spend it all, shoot it, play it, lose it, all, right away, every time. Do not hoard what seems good for a later place in the book, or for another book; give it, give it all, give it now. The impulse to save something for a better place later is the signal to spend it now.

Something more will arise for later, something better. These things fill from behind, from beneath, like well water. Similarly, the impulse to keep to yourself what you have learned is not only shameful, it is destructive. Anything you do not give freely and abundantly becomes lost to you. You open your safe and find ashes.[1]

Above all, we see that it was not Jesus' death that vanquished the final enemy in this conflict, but Jesus' life. It was not his death alone that was his vocation; the whole of his life constitutes his response to God's call. Jesus, in his self-centeredness, gave himself over fully to life. He was in full possession of himself. And when he gave himself over fully to life, he released his life as gift. Once loosed, the gift was beyond the bounds of legal ownership. It was—and is—free. In this offering of self, Jesus realized—made real—the fullness of God's will for human being, so far as we can discern that will.

And in this offering, though his life was literally beyond his control, he was no less centered in himself. In other words, Jesus was the incarnation of human integrity: at one and the same time self-centered and freely given. But such integrity is not come by easily, neither is it easily maintained. Like life itself, this integrity is dynamic: constantly tempted, constantly offered.

It is not the struggle to die or to face death that marks Jesus as unique. Many before and since have undertaken that challenge, some with even greater dignity and grace than Jesus. No, what sets him apart is his struggle to give his life—actually to make a gift of his life. This is the struggle of vocation—to be a cross maker.

A cross is only the intersection of two lines, one vertical and the other horizontal. To live on the intersection of those lines, however, is literally to cross over the lines that separate one from the other. We want to live on either one plane or the other, but not at the intersection. We want each secluded from the other, and strict order maintained between them.

To give our life over to the chaos, to the unknown, is to cross over and become a cross maker. To give our life over to others, and to God, and as a gift to ourselves is to cross over the lines and become a cross maker. To cross our own boundaries and give life over—this is the vocation of the cross maker, the path Jesus shows us.

The ultimate vocational struggle of the cross maker, then, is to cross the final boundary of self and enter into the openness of life in all its fullness. This is the boundary that separates us from the fullness of life, the very one that separates life from us and holds it away. To cross it is to enter life's fullness and allow the fullness of life to enter and take over our own lives. This should sound more than vaguely familiar to the Christian who regularly prays that Christ "may live in us, and we in him." In this eucharistic devotional prayer, we are invited to ingest bread and wine, the body and blood of Jesus, into ourselves. It is an invitation to Jesus to cross our boundaries: the symbolic ingestion of his "body" and his most vital "body fluid" is a willing invasion, even contamination, of ourselves.

This is our ultimate challenge: to cease our insatiable desire for control over our lives, in our lives. To step down from that place from which we rule over our lives, to step down from that place from which we attempt to rule over the lives of God and neighbor, exerting our own control—to step down from that throne of personal empire, and offer our life, our self, as gift.

And offering one's life as gift means surrendering it, not in resignation, but in desire. It is not an act of submission, but an act of offering. This was the struggle that wrenched the final week of Jesus' life, that sent temple tables flying, caused a fig tree to wither and die, enraged authorities, confused friends, and brought Jesus to his knees in Gethsemane.

How could he not be conflicted? He was locked in that ultimate human struggle. He prayed not for the obliteration of his will, but for the reconciliation of his will. He did not ask God to take his will from him. He asked God to bring it into conformity with the divine will. It was not sovereignty he sought, but partnership.

From the beginning of Israel's recorded life and perhaps even beyond, we have known instinctively and perceptively of a will beyond ourselves whose character is experienced as prodigal offering. All we have ever known is its singular devotion to us: I shall be your God, you shall be my people. To be called into conformity with that will is to be called into its eternal offertory. In giving freely and willingly, we do that will. This was what Jesus fervently prayed for in the garden.

Jesus responded to the call to live the very fullness of life for which we all were created. He did not live for us in any vicarious sense. He was not a sacrifice to God's ambition—like someone who subverts his own will to follow the path of others' expectations or demands. Jesus' courageous offering is not a substitute for our own responsibility. No one can have your vocation for you. Jesus was and is the incarnation of God's image and intention for human being. He is the will of God discernible in the human frame.

Only to live. This was his unique vocation: to live. We do not come into relationship with Jesus by his teaching or his healing, his political organizing or his theological ruminations. It is neither by his words, nor simply by his deeds, but rather by the totality of his living—and most particularly, his specific living in those brief latter and public years of his life—that any have come to know of him.

He was not a writer. No papers, no recordings survive—only a few fragments, none of which he authored. In truth, he was not even much of a "doer," for when we examine his life it is remarkably unproductive by our standards. There are no verifiable artifacts, unless one counts the shreds of cloth reputed to be his shroud, or a splinter from ancient wood thought to be his cross. Nothing tangible that can be held in our hands. No political philosophy survives, no institutional organization, for he espoused none.

The only product that remains from his lifetime is himself. He is known and recognized far beyond all our attempts to contain him. He is democrat and communist, of no color and every color. All that remains is an inherited perspective that cannot be other than relationship. All that remains is this person, Jesus, whose life exists only in relationship to another, like me or you.

In truth, he can be found nowhere else, much to the frustration of all who would locate the historical Jesus in time and space, and let him remain there. His vocation, so far as I can discern, was simply to be. That he fulfilled that vocation I can only attest to through my profound experience that he is.

Jesus is, for me, as the late "Mama" Cass Eliot sang of him in lyric and tune that linger in my memory as fresh as when I first heard them:

One time I trusted a stranger
Cuz I heard his sweet song
And it was gently encitin' me
Tho' there was somethin' wrong
But when I turned he was gone.
Blindin' me his song remain remindin' me
He's a bandit and a heartbreaker
Oh, Jesus was a cross maker.[2]

Jesus is a cross maker. He is a bandit and a heart-breaker—an outlaw who challenges, even flaunts, our boundaries. To love him shatters the boundary of the heart itself. He engages us in that ultimate struggle. His very existence challenges our every excuse and encourages us to move beyond the status quo.

But the way of his vocation was not smooth. Neither is ours. "Only after the writer lets literature shape her can she perhaps shape literature," writes Annie Dillard of her own profession. In describing the vocation of the artist, she gives expression to a reality we all share:

> In working class France, when an apprentice got hurt, or when he got tired, the experienced workers said, "It is the trade entering his body." The art must enter the body, too. A painter cannot use paint like glue or screws to fasten down the world. The tubes of paint are like fingers; they work only if, inside the painter, the neural pathways are wide and clear to the brain. Cell by cell, molecule by molecule, atom by atom, part of the brain changes physical shape to accommodate and fit paint.

You adapt yourself, Paul Klee said, to the contents of the paintbox. Adapting yourself to the contents of the paintbox, he said, is more important than nature and its study. The painter, in other words, does not fit the paints to the world. He most certainly does not fit the world to himself. He fits himself to the paint. The self is the servant who bears the paintbox and its inherited contents.[3]

This is what Jesus confronted in that final week in Jerusalem. Perhaps it was the work of his entire lifetime. But it was most evident in those last days of his life as the struggle between his will to control and his will to give locked in mortal embrace. It is no less true for us: to engage this struggle is to die. We use the metaphor of death so easily in liturgy. We speak in measured cadences of dying and rising.

But it is hard, this trade entering our bodies. It is hard, the fullness of human being such as we know in Jesus battering at our pitiful clenchings, our brave little strainings to maintain our hold over ourselves. And when Jesus finally prevails, that heartbreaker, we do die. And no metaphorical death, either. Only then do we appreciate the place of resurrection in our own vocation.

The vocation of Jesus extended beyond his physical death. That is the message of the resurrection. I take this to mean not that death is our vocation, but that death is only a part of our living. As our hymnody, liturgy, and scriptures proclaim, death is not the final word. The story does go on.

Of the details of physical resurrection I have no need, and little interest. All that matters is that in his living, Jesus gives us tangible assurance that it is to life that we are called, even though that life leads us through death. I find no affinity with those who maintain that Jesus "gave himself up to death." Jesus gave himself to life, of which death is certainly a part.

Jesus gave himself to life and thus crossed over the boundary we have made of death. For though death itself is made of God's creation, death as a boundary is of *our* making, not God's. If Jesus' resurrection means anything, it means that giving oneself to life is a gift that extends beyond the limitation of our sensate experience that terminates in death. This is an important component in our meditation upon vocation, for it suggests that our call is not to performance or accomplishment. It is a call to relationship.

If our call extended merely to performance, death would surely mark our end, for the very meaning of the word "performance" and its synonym "accomplishment" is "to fill up, to complete." But when Jesus uttered the words, "It is finished," he was as wrong and as mistaken as when he uttered the question, "Why have you forsaken me?" Surely, these utterances from the cross were of similar character. God did not forsake Jesus. And it was not finished, not by a long shot.

Vocation is more than the fulfillment of days or tasks. Long after I can no longer do those things by which my accomplishment is measured, I shall not cease to be. Comforting as this realization might be to me in times of extremity or duress, this realization is particularly important to me here and now. It is important—perhaps even essential—to know that my vocation is not measured in accomplishment, that it is never truly finished.

Forty days after Easter we commemorate the resurrected Jesus' physical departure from earth. I am especially fond of Luke's account of the ascension because of its simplicity. The rendering in the *New English Bible* is my favorite:

> [Jesus] led them out as far as Bethany, and blessed them with uplifted hands; and in the act of blessing he parted from them. And they

returned to Jerusalem with great joy, and spent
all their time in the temple praising God.
(Luke 24:50-53)

"In the act of blessing he parted from them." A
blessing is a divine favor, a bestowing of happiness or
prosperity, a gift. The parting *is* the blessing; his leav-
ing *is* the gift. How else to explain the disciples'
uncharacteristic response to such an abrupt abandon-
ment: "They returned to Jerusalem with great joy, and
spent all their time in the temple praising God." They
had just lost their friend, companion, guide, teacher,
and savior. Yet they were filled with joy, praising God.

Perhaps they were filled with joy because their
lives were again fully their own. They had been given
the gift of self, and of one another. They were fully
responsible; they had cares to share, problems to challenge them to their best efforts and engage their full
attention.

If Jesus is the new Adam, then the ascension,
angels and all, is the moment when humanity is
restored to the garden, welcomed back into full partnership with God's creative activity. The supreme act
of divine favor is this letting go—God's trust in us evi-
denced in Jesus' departure from the world. The
supreme blessing is this gift of complete trust. The

ascension is God's affirmation of trust in us, God's affirmation of love for us, God's affirmation of hope for us and our world. The ascension is the mass ordination of all ministries—all our unique ministries—for we are all ministers serving the priesthood of God, Creator of all.

"In the act of blessing he parted from them." They were on their own, restored to full partnership with God. Their adventures, their lives, were not ending but beginning. No wonder they were filled with joy.

Endnotes

1. Annie Dillard, *The Writing Life* (New York: Harper & Row, 1989), 69.
2. Judee Sill, "Jesus was a Cross Maker," © 1971 April-Blackwood Music (BMI), *Cass Eliot*, RCA Victor LSP0-4619.
3. Dillard, *The Writing Life*, 69.